ISBN: 1-886895-16-3
$5.95
Limited edition
Copyright 1998
Poetry Harbor
Post Office Box 103
Duluth, Minnesota 55801-0103

Artist Photograph by Sister Joyce Fournier.
Cover Art by Pat Hagen.

This chapbook was made possible, in part, by a grant from the Arrowhead Regional Arts Council, with funding provided by the Minnesota State Legislature, and by Poetry Harbor Members.

Acknowledgements: *Atlanta Review, WolfHead Quarterly, The Christian Century, North Coast Review, Christian Science Monitor, Harvard Divinity School of Feminist Studies.*

Special Thanks to:
    Pat Hagen, Sharon Hill, Connie Wanek, Todd White, John Hinkle, and patrick mckinnon.
Cover layout and printing by Tight Squeak Press.

A Creature Who Belongs

Nancy Fitzgerald

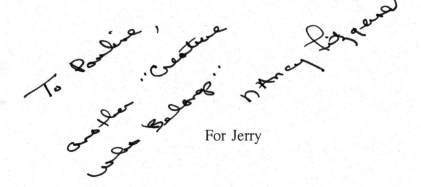

For Jerry

Barley

I begin with barley,
peel and chop the onion,
toss in tomatoes, garlic -
turn it on to simmer,
and set out for a walk.

At first I think of work.
The pace, the rush,
and what comes next. But
when we turn toward home,
the dog bounds up with a stick,
demands a toss and turns
my thoughts to soup.

How when I lift the lid
its breath will rise and
the pearly barley
will be plump and firm.
How oregano and maybe thyme
and hunks of bread and candlelight,
how grains, and herbs and animals
will blend and mend most days.

Bridal Boutique

My daughter, bride to be, slips off her shorts
at the bridal boutique, glides in wearing gown
number one. I sit among mothers, watching
dresses float by like silk swans on a pond.

Sequins and pearls shimmer on satin.
Rhinestones and crystals glisten on
billowy folds of glossy soft silk.
Bodices beaded, lacy and scalloped,
trains fall in ripples of tulle and net.
Each bride to be steps up on the platform,
tucks in her tummy, turns toward the
mirror with a critical eye.

The sales woman hovers close by.
"Every girl deserves cleavage on
her wedding day" she adds in a pad
"These flowers draw the eye away from the hips.
Notice how this one elongates the torso.
See how these sleeves broaden the shoulders"
She ruffles the rump, "no need for the bustle"
she glides between the brides.
"Satin may be a little too clingy. Try this
it wraps and creates a slender effect."
The brides peck and preen, dropping dresses like
feathers, molting in wingbeats of self disapproval.

My daughter emerges in a body skimming sheath.
I hold my breath. The gown is spectacular.
Long clean lines cling to her curves,
layers of organza fall gently at her knees,
it is elegant, fluid, mermaidish and sexy.
The clerk's eye is sharp as a hawk.
"It needs only slight alteration.
A bit too tight right here, just over the hips."
She flips up the hem to look at the seams.

The bride stands like a lily, a slight
slender stalk. "I'll go on a diet there's
plenty of time to loose all this fat."
I close my eyes and see swans -
shimmering flocks, graceful and strong.
"We'll alter the dress. Your body's just fine."
Me the old trumpeter of truth.

Places

All three of my children
live in places I haven't been.
I can't picture how the light
surrounds them as they sit
and read or where the fridge
or stove are placed, or when
they eat or sleep, or just
how the phone is sitting
when it rings and their
recorded voices answer
in the empty space.

In the West of Ireland, mothers
who had never been to Dublin
came to think of Boston as
"just a parish over."
Studying the horizon,
they must have ached until
they threw off aprons,
put out fires, locked doors
and crossed the sea to see

the slant of light, the hyacinths,
the neighborhoods where their
children lived. Once home
they blessed the ordinary
as their kettles whistled
in the evening dusk.

Light and Darkness

Who will get the Kollwitz
mother with dead child,
the broadside, the oil
woman in the tub,
the watercolor orchards
in the sun, the Watanabe
Christ? Shall I designate
or let the children choose
which patterns, textures,
truths, which shadows,
lights and darks they want
to hang up from their past?

Swimming With My Daughter

I was floating in the sun
close to shore when she said,
"Mom I'm going to the island."
I flipped and followed
her strong, easy glide
wondering if I could make it
through strong currents
and over choppy waves.
Though I swam hard,
she stayed out ahead.

Resting on the pier
I measured how the wind
had softened and how I
could float if necessary
easing the return.
I refrained from asking her
to swim back side by side,
to follow just in case.

My own mother did not
make the call to tell me
it was time.
It was up to me to see
the ebbing tide,
that she was sinking,
needed help across
to the other side.

This time I'm safe on shore.
She wrings out her dark hair,
adjusts her suit and walks
toward town.
I sit and watch the boats bob,
look back at what a long way
I have come.

Mammogram

"O moon above the mountain rim,
please shine a little further on my path."
                Isumi Shikibu (947-1034)

"This lump is well defined
we can tell it is a cyst."
She points to splotches
on the x-ray of my breasts.
Each new moon I touch them,
know their curves and crescents,
catch and count their contours in my dreams.

When mother's lump went crazy,
wild in her lymph nodes,
she hardly spoke of death,
but wept about her legacy to me.

Once more I have been released
from what I fear. I want to hike
and camp along a canyon rim,
sail out past the island
with a friend, bring cherry
blossoms in the house,
try a recipe for creme brulee.

"O moon. . .
shine a little further on my path."

Zion Canyon

The Indians stopped
at the mouth of the canyon -
a place too sacred to enter,
where the winds blew the dunes
for thousands of years
into natural temples of god.

We step lightly up the rocky ledge,
past pinyon pine, juniper and cactus
sip wine at sunset on the rim,
talk of work and love and then
as shadows fill the valley,
I ask about your friend.
"She is tired" you say, "of illness
and of struggle. She has her bone
marrow cleansed tomorrow."

I have known for years
how to fling a prayer across a lake,
to send it out and name the names
skipping them like stones across the surface,
but I have never prayed in canyons.

We move closer to the edge
and call her name.
Our voices float
from wall to wall
circling the rocks,
echoing our prayer,
coming back to us,
deeper than we spoke
daring us to hope.

Sierra Nevadas

My body fits
into the crevice
of these rocks.
I stretch out.
Their warmth,
the rushing river
flush winter
from my bones.

I am not a visitor
a tourist,
I am a creature
who belongs.
Jay, squirrel, coyote,
fish, lizard, self.

Epiphany

Deep in December dreams of pageants past,
I awoke to an empty creche,
put seed out for the chickadee,
set suet for the woodpecker
brewed coffee for the two of us
as we got lost in leisure.

Later at the kitchen window,
three plumed kings arrived.
First the Downy, white and black,
his small red patch flamed
against the morning snow.
Then the Hairy, wary, wild,
flicked his needle beak into the suet,
bowed his head, his crimson beauty spot
blazed between the birches.

Then the drumming and the chirping ceased,
the juncos stopped their scratching.
In swept the Pileated,
his brilliant crest erect,
his tuft a diadem,
his gift a jeweled cap,
his gift an Awakening.

The Meaning of Life

There is a moment just before
a dog vomits when its stomach
heaves dry, pumping what's deep
inside the belly to the mouth.
If you are fast you can grab
her by the collar and shove her
out the door, avoid the slimy bile
from landing on the floor.
You must be quick, decisive,
controlled, and if you miss
the cue and the dog erupts
en route, you must forgive
her quickly and give your
self to scrubbing up the mess.

Most of what I have learned
in life leads back to this.

Swerve

How do you write a poem about a dog
whose attentive, furry head was hit
by a speeding car before the sun
came up, while he walked with you
to get the morning paper.

How do you set it down that since
the children left, he climbed
the totem pole to your heart,
that when you spoke to him,
he sat studying your face
and you felt contained.
That hiking in the woods with him
no matter what the weather
became a covenant.

How do you tell about his black lab
friend who sniffed the bloody snow,
now comes back every day, accepts your
hand upon his head, but looks beyond
into the house, his tail still,
his silent eyes a question.

How do you say that losing him
leaves a void like living without
music and that the squirrels
have taken over, swinging at the feeder
and that the only way to end this poem
is stop.

Rescue

When I heard about the pills she took
how she'd walked into the woods alone
I wondered if she'd worn her boots,
a hat, her gloves and if the trees had
felt her warmth, her heartbeat
in their marrow as she curled
at their roots in the snow to die.

Days before we had leaned against
some trunks and felt them sway
into our spines. I hoped they
might quiet her, but the wind
was high and fierce above and
as they cracked she spoke
with fear of depression,
insomnia, a self she didn't know.

When they found her in the woods,
the spot beneath the aspens
where she dropped was thawed
almost to the earth
from her body's warmth.

As spring rains came
her imprint in the snow,
the footprints of the rescue team
melted in the ground and disappeared
as though such darkness must be left behind
for sap to run, and for the birch to grow.

The Seven Sorrows

1. Keeping Vigil in the I.C.U.

After nine hours of surgery
you lay stapled, strapped,
red from blood
yellow with iodine,
tubed, monitored, shuddering
amidst the others moaning, heaving,
wrestling with the angels down in Sheol.
Up until that time
you said you'd be fine
and I believed you.

Now your eyes
which had always steadied mine
looked out in terror.

I held your feet and read the Psalms.
"If I make my bed in Sheol God is there"
"God's heart is the first to break"
"No coward Soul is mine"
The lies I learned to live by.

2. Waiting for Reports

The sounds of nurses
some with wings,
some thumped and banged,
attentive tuned listening for the god
the doctor, the savior,
the brisk clip of his footstep
the bevy at his heels.
He did not look at me,
but fussed around the bed,
that high altar where you lay
in pain, waiting, waiting,
for reports.

3. Crying in the Tub

At home you sat soaking in the tub.
I brought a candle and sherry,
Sought your eyes.
You held the glass to toast us.
The beauty of your body bruised,
The steam, the sherry, our love.

4. Toxins in the Brain

When the toxins hit his brain
he went wild.
Restless, tormented,
wandered through the house
like a muddled bear, turned
the kitchen faucet on,
stood shuffling there.
I followed him deep,
deep into this cave,
calling to the one he was before.
But he was gone.

5. Days of Stupor

The radio played Bach
as he journeyed out
toward the other side
held captive by his body.
Hours and days of silence,
then his eyes sought mine,
"That's a Bach Cantata in
D Minor."

6. The Gentle Firemen Arrive

Downstairs once too often
for a meal
we could not get him up again.
The firemen came quickly,
picked him up right
in his chair and carried him to bed.
They tucked him tenderly.
"Thank you, gentlemen" he said.
They stood silent in the sadness.

7. Helping to Open the Door

"Help me open the door, Help Me,
Help me end this agony."
"I cannot."
More morphine, more morphine more
some water from the cup
to your lips to my lips
someone on the other side
hear our plea, please
hear our plea.

It's Time

Now I go there alone in sorrow
to the house where you died.

I sort and toss
the evidence of your life,
papers, books,
old files, letters,
model boats,
kits you never built,
photos plaques and honors.
The dust of it,
the work of it,
what to save or throw.

In a dream room
your corpse lay white,
uncovered.
I forgot to bury you
and now it's time.

What old pain needs gathering
What festering images
Which suitcase for the spirit
Which seven sorrows?

March 29, 1985

He died the same night as Chagall,
floated up away from her
as she tried to anchor him
with a final kiss.

Now in racing skies she sees
acrobats in slants of white,
lovers drifting in the trees,
scarlet angels, flying fish,
vases full of flower moons,
swimmers in a sea of blossoms,
levitating brides and grooms.

When she sleeps the purple village
rests beneath white lily stars.
Crested roosters watch at dawn
as cubes of morning light arise.

Time Out

*"...but I might learn something of mindlessness,
something of the purity of living in the physical senses."*
                                    Annie Dillard

1. Seals

On rocky shelves just off the coast,
seals lounge like long sleek logs
along the ledge. A mother snuggles
with her pup, brushing his small face
with her whiskered snout.
As the tide comes in, they roll,
flap and slide into the water
dive and fish, bobbing round
eyed in the sea.

I am happy keeping watch,
counting noses while they swim,
noting how they paddle back and
hoist their slippery bodies
with their flippers.
They settle on the rocks
warmed by the sun.
I stretch out
and sleep.

2. Sage

On the reservation by the River Animas
I find wild sage, cut and bundle it,
brush our faces with its soft leaves,
set it in the sun. It permeates our days.
Smelling it we remember wild horses
running in formation on the desert,
Veronica, speaking Ute to lizards.
When it dries, it turns brittle.
I light its tips, smudge the air,
and multiply my praise.

3. Dog Fur

I have always lived with dogs
and loved their fur.
One more silky than the rest
let me weep on him and often
carried grief deep in his pelt.
This new dog's coat is energetic,
woolly, wiry. It springs back
from brushing, invigorates the hands.
When I can, I touch him twenty times a day.

4. Coffee

Mornings after his death
dreaming grey
slumped in bed,
sleet sliding down the pane,
there was coffee.

The bag of beans
the aromatic hit,
grinding, brewing,
the taste and then
the lift up from the pit,
the eggshell walk on hope.

5. Music

At another campfire
two women drum.
There is no tune, no harmony
just the slap of skin on skin.
I feel the ancient flickerings,
leave my fire and move to them.

Tracks on the Trail

How good it is
the solitude of winter
to see tracks on the trail.

My snowshoes containing
their own daily rhythm
keep the long white

path packed and open.
Snow falls so deep on
either side to stumble

is to trap a leg,
perhaps to freeze
there among the

birch and
aspen bent
beneath the weight.

Dog, fox, deer,
paw and foot
foot and paw

prints under
and on top
of mine.

Sunday Morning in June

In a marshy place,
in a ferny bog
by the balsam
and the cedar trees
clumped among the cattails
Showy Lady Slippers
pop their small pink
pockets in such profusion
no one can count them.

I want to sit
at this oracle,
among the lavender,
among the orchids,
singing in the
swampy shrine,
singing of the
sacred rising
of the pink.

Monarch

We were in the valley
cutting wood for winter
when you slipped silently
from your chrysalis, leaving
it lifeless on the twig.

You rested at our table,
spreading and closing your
brilliant orange, opening
and closing, the black
tracery, the white dots,
catching sunlight,
your wings illuminated
like parchment on an
ancient manuscript.

You finished fanning, the
breeze scooped you from
my hand and for days
we watched every monarch
gliding by for your orange
by chance, your radiance.

Wild Turkeys

My hound, head down
nose to the ground
runs in circles
dizzy with the scent
of wild turkeys. They
strutted there across
the field before she
was up, then flew
into the brush and
disappeared.

To see God they
tell you to meditate,
be alert to mystery,
keep your eyes open
not just to what's
in front of you,
but what's flown away
or burrowed deep.
There at the edges -
up or maybe down.

The King of Dung

He said two paleontologists in Canada
found a piece of dung from a dinosaur
seventeen feet long and four feet wide
and that they could tell it was a Rex
who dropped it. They knew it ate its
mammal prey in a vicious way from the
bones crushed in excrement. He said
for a creature big as a locomotive
to feed with that anatomy would be
like a human trying to eat enough
with a pin point mouth and a straw like
neck. He said the dung would go on tour
to museums across the country and now
hordes of little boys calcified in line
will wait with parents waiting,
waiting for a peek at the King of Dung.

Old Women

When I was twenty in Yugoslavia
I saw old women dressed in black
walking on the dusty road,
carrying sticks to prod their
ambling cows. I hardly noticed
searching in cathedrals,
drinking late in beer halls,
flinging my own emptiness,
watching for some giant call
to summon me. They seemed
narrow as their waists,
fixed in time.

When I was fifty visiting Crete,
I saw old women leading goats
from villages to graze in family plots.
This time I looked more closely.
One in rubber boots, her back
curved like the sickle in her
weathered hands, cut greens and
put them in a basket made of vines.
Evenings, babushkas drawn across their
foreheads, they walked side by side
to fetch their friendly beasts,
their aprons loose, their smiles
and their pockets deep and wide.

We May Move To Crete

We may move to Crete and live
among the pomegranate trees,
see their scarlet flowers bloom
in spring and learn the ancient way
to break its fruit on New Year's day
across the threshold of our hut,
to count the juicy seeds inside
as blessings for our lives.

We may move to Crete and watch wind
wave through the olive trees,
learn to press the fruit,
dip bread, cook purple plants,
drizzle salads in its oil
suck olives in the orchard,
make tapenade and tarts.
We may light lamps, make wreaths,
crown our roof with olive branches.

We may move to Crete and sit
beneath the sacred myrtle tree,
use its bark to make perfume,
press its berries to drink,
pick its bursting blossoms
pass bouquets to old dark women
passing with their tethered goats.

We may move to Crete, and wade
in streams beside the fig trees,
lean against their polished trunks,
fan our faces with their leaves,
gather them to eat with grapes,
dried to mix with nuts and cake,
smother them in cream and honey,
dizzy in the sweetness of their seed.

If we move to Crete, we'll plant
a cypress tree and wait for it
to fling its knarled limbs
across the rocky hill, then
prune it carefully and carve
small offerings to the goddess
Aphrodite, worshipped
since antiquity in Crete.

And if we only dream of Crete
from these bare hills
on frozen nights
the birch will stand immaculate
against the snow, white on white.

Who Taught You Rapture?

Rembrandt's spots of light
Mozart's violin chasing the piano
the grain of oak awakening to oil
the indigo returning in the spring
the dance as a woman's skirt moves
across her thighs and her partner
catches all her ripples in his arms
the baby wet and warm from birth
resting after labor on your tummy
the rain
the wren
the work
the blossoming fruit
the day in bed alone
the day in bed together
the dog running down the beach
the poem opening like a rose
a taste of honey in Crete
your mother's lap
your father's laugh
the pancakes made for you
the silent night
the ease of death
the snowy trail
the summer sun
the risen loaf
the perfect sail
the silent night
the stars
the breath
the moon
the silence
who taught you rapture?

About the Author:

Nancy Fitzgerald's poetry and short stories have been published in numerous literary magazines including *Sisters Today, North Coast Review, Atlanta Review, Mother Superior* and *WolfHead Quarterly*. She participated in the Tweed Museum Broadside Series in 1996, collaborating with visual artist Catherine Koemptgen. For many years, Nancy has been an integral and important member of Northern Minnesota's thriving literary scene. This is her second collection, the first being, An Inward Turning Out (Poetry Harbor 1994). She currently resides on the rural edge of Duluth overlooking Lake Superior in a beautiful house with her husband Jerry and their dog.